MW00476126

readings from the book of exile

readings from the book of exile
Pádraig Ó Tuama

CANTERBURY
PRESS
Norwich

© Pádraig Ó Tuama 2012
All poems © Pádraig Ó Tuama

First published in 2012 by the Canterbury Press Norwich
Editorial office
3rd Floor Invicta House,
108–114 Golden Lane,
London, EC1Y 0TG, UK

Canterbury Press is an imprint of Hymns Ancient & Modern Ltd
(a registered charity)
13A Hellesdon Park Road, Norwich,
Norfolk, NR6 5DR, UK

www.canterburypress.co.uk

All rights reserved. No part of this publication may be reproduced,
stored in a retrieval system, or transmitted,
in any form or by any means, electronic, mechanical,
photocopying or otherwise, without the prior permission of
the publisher, Canterbury Press.

The Author has asserted his right under the Copyright,
Designs and Patents Act, 1988,
to be identified as the Author of this Work

British Library Cataloguing in Publication data

A catalogue record for this book is available
from the British Library

978 1 84825 205 9

Originated by The Manila Typesetting
Printed and bound in Great Britain by
CPI Group (UK) Ltd., Croydon, CR0 4YY

Contents

A reading from the book of exile, chapter one   1
Deoraíocht (Exile)   2
Narrative theology # 1   4
Circle   5
And even though you do not know your name   6
Affirmative action   8

A reading from the book of exile, chapter two   9
Narrative theology # 2   10
In-between the sun and moon   12
Tortuous atonement   13
Four poems at Easter   14
This strange country   21

A reading from the book of exile, chapter three   23
L is for Lonely   24
The beginning of wisdom   26
Flesh of my flesh   27
Northeast morning roads of home   28
'Tis the gift   29
Of skinny dipping   30

A reading from the book of exile, chapter four   33
Creed   34
The visit of the queen of the lesbians   36
A song of ascent   38
Dominic and Jenny's sex life   40
Howth's soft heather   42
Mo sheasamh ort, lá na choise tinne   44

A reading from the book of exile, chapter five   47
My love is a wide wide ocean   48
Ar eagla na heagla   49
Solitary flights   50
Mourning prayer   52
Binding the void with a name   55
An offering to God in exile   57

A reading from the book of exile,
the unwritable chapter   60
Untitled # 1   61
Till death do us part   62
Intercession for lesbian and gay Ugandans   63
Postcards to a dead friend   65
September the twelfth two thousand and one   66
Marbh is imithe ar mean lá an t-samhraidh   68
Untitled # 2   70

A reading from the book of exile, chapter six   71
A circle keeps beginning. A circle is unending.   72
Fashion the world   73
Shhhhh   74
What I needed to hear   75
Narrative theology # 3   76
Hold yourself together and pull yourself apart   77

While he was in Malta 79

Who do you say that I am? 81

Ar scáth a chéile a mhaireas na daoine 83

The task is ended 84

Dedication

Do mo PD, Le grá mór

A reading from the book of exile
chapter one

there are no chapters

Deoraíocht* (Exile)

And their god was carved
from their own hollow breathing
their toil was hard
their babies born grieving.
Clothed with desire
they continued believing
that their lives began
with their edenic leaving.

And he's afraid.
And he will fear.
And he is hiding.
And he is here.

Their path was worn
as the furnace was yawning
they slept in the evening
they spoke in the dawning.
She was the mother
of all that was breathing.
He was the earth
and she was his reason.

And she's afraid.
And she will fear.

---

* The Irish word for Exile is 'Deoraíocht', which carries the implication 'to
be in a state of tears'.

And she is hiding.
And she is here.

They came from nothing
so the nothing came with them.
Their chaos lay open
and their chaos played with them.

And they're afraid.
And they will fear.
And they are hiding.
And they are here.

They move between
cunning and exposure
sometimes one answer, sometimes many,
sometimes silence, never closer.

And we're afraid.
And we fear.
And we are hiding.
And we are here.

Narrative theology # 1
(for Peter Saunders)

And I said to him
Are there answers to all of this?
And he said
The answer is in a story
and the story is being told.

And I said
But there is so much pain
And she answered, plainly,
Pain will happen.

Then I said
Will I ever find meaning?
And they said
You will find meaning
Where you give meaning.

The answer is in the story
And the story isn't finished.

Circle
(for Dani)

It's funny how things come in
circles.
You, sitting on a step,
smoking a cigarette,
watching leaves fall off a
slowly stripping tree.
Me, hanging photos on a wall,
including one of you
receiving, like a priestess,
your lover's confession.
Me telling stories of
your conversations.
You, weeping
when your dad asked you
how you were.
Me writing poems about life
while I was slowly plunging into
death.
You breathing in those
same lines,
sitting on a step,
smoking a cigarette.

And even though you do not know your name

And even though
you do not know your name
you have given nameless places
recognition.
You have baptised spaces merely by
inhabitation,
there has been an inner invitation
that you've accepted,
with all that holy, wholly hesitation.

Leaving others back
behind the curtain,
you've asserted something
in the face of god-divine,
something you were finding out,
a kind of
leave-it-all-behind-and-mind-you-don't-feel-guilty
sense of declaration.

And even though
you do not know your name,
your inhabitation space was named
by face-to-facing something that
you met and listened to.

This space is yours,
whatever it is called,
named by life and all this living,
and all the best things that regret can bring
and all the hope you muster.

Affirmative action

In the Irish language, there is not a word for 'yes'. There is not a word for 'no' either.

You can only answer in the affirmative – you can say 'I will', or 'I won't'. You can say 'I can'. You can say 'I am' or 'I am not'.

It is appropriate that a language so poetic as to suggest a bridge between the word for exile and the word for weeping would be rooted in an earthy solidity that requires answers to be linked to an action. Affirmative answers are indicated by action.

Let your yes be yes and your no be no.

Let your yes be seen in your doing.

Let your no be not-doing.

If you say yes, but do-not-do, it is a no.

So, forget all your talk.

Tell me by what you do.

A reading from the book of exile
chapter two

he has been moved beyond belief

Narrative theology # 2

I used to need to know
the end of every story
but these days I only
need the start to get me going.

God is the crack
where the story begins.
We are the crack
where the story gets interesting

We are the choice of
where to begin –
the person going out?
the stranger coming in?

God is the fracture,
and the ache in your voice,
God is the story
flavoured with choice

God is the pillar of salt
full of pity
accusing God
for the sulphurous city.

God is the woman who bleeds
and who touches.
We are the story
of courage or blushes.

God is the story
of whatever works.
God is the twist at the end
and the quirks.

We are the start,
and we are the centre,
we're the characters,
narrators, inventors.

God is the bit
that we can't explain –
maybe the healing
maybe the pain.

We are the bit
that God can't explain
maybe the harmony
maybe the strain.

God is the plot,
and we are the writers,
the story of winners
and the story of fighters,

the story of love,
and the story of rupture,
the story of stories,
the story without structure.

In-between the sun and moon

In-between the sun and moon,
I sit and watch
and make some room
for letting light and twilight mingle,
shaping hope
and making single glances last eternity,
a little more,
extending love beyond the doors of welcoming,
while wedding all the parted people,
even sons to violent mothers,
and searching all the others finding light
where twilight lingers,
in-between the sun and moon.

Tortuous atonement

Do you like the smell of tortured Jesus
burning the snow?
Do you like how his veins are pulsing
underneath his ripped skin's glow?
Do you salivate and lick your lips,
swallowing your spit,
imagining the sweet meat taste
from the barbecuing pit?
Do you drink the drink and talk the talk
inviting all your friends,
To bask in resurrection scents
and eat the flesh of all amends?

Four poems at Easter

(i) Holy Thursday

Some flapping friars, frocked in
white and flowing garments
billowed at the evening's awning
as I stole past
and found my half way seat
[not too near the front – I need to know behind me
not too near the back, I want to see the priests]
A rare and lovely moment happened –
an inner calm calling me to gentle prayer –
crystal voices singing with
violins crooning chords to beloved hymns.

A young fellow, sixteen or so,
sitting two pews in front of me,
wore a blue t-shirt that said:
'smile if you're a wanker'.
A young woman,
one pew in front of me,
sat and cried
the whole way through –
quietly, with two pink roses in her hair.

The shy and awkward priest washed
the feet of the pre-selected
disciples, while the
eloquent and prophet-eyed orator

spoke cleverly to the gathered
about feasts – little and large
and little again.
Pointing, perhaps, to all the little Easters,
on the days between our Friday and Good Sundays.

A beaming, waif-like lady
smiled the holy host
from its holder to my
waiting palm.
While she looked exhausted
she twinkled eyes towards me.

And finally, they processed out,
the solemn friars, not flapping now,
floating towards the door,
with us, the brave,
us the faithful,
us the wise and noble,
us the broken, bent and backwards.
We the needy and the lonely
left quietly row by row.

(ii) Good Friday

The light looked in the
sunstained windows,
carved by careful hands
with crafted instruments,
like a locked-out lover
lamenting his lost key.

The soon-to-be Easter light
flooded the space between
the tenth and eleventh stations
the stripping and the
nailing at twelve o'clock,

highlighted the night between
our fallings and our flyings
on this Friday of our good sorrows,
or bad sorrows

our mad, and sad,
and
glad that there are gladder days beyond these days
sorrows.

We toast the night, o felix culpa,
and hide the light of lights

for a while.

(iii) Vigil

A tram clanked by and saw
firelit people
celebrate the light
on a dark March evening
huddled round a hobo's fire
breathing in the air of sharing.

Later, following a solemn march
to a church of shadowed arches
to hear readings from history's pages,
a bell was rung
and then again, and again,
proclaiming peace for these
chimneyed houses of our
inelegant suburbs.

And light is falling, dawning,
going, flowing, showing, moving, wooing,
gushing, roaring, spouting, rolling down
flooding spaces and birthing hidden
corners
with beauty of a gorgeous kind.

My protestant friend beside me
cannot take communion
but we shared a peaceful silence
at gentle harmonies
and sung three-tiered responses
to century's prayers.

A tram ride later,
we shared mountain bread
with soft white cheese and tea
at the only open street café.

(iv) Bethlehem, Easter 2002

Arrived, in a dark
pitching, two thousand and
two wintertimes ago.

Warmed by animal heat
and the nighttime sweat of
his exhausted mother,

surrounded by angels,
singing peace and pleasure
to all who follow,

while timid shepherds bring
kind gifts – a lamb, a reassurance –
a gentle prophecy
for long years ahead.

And now, huddled in
the hidden corners of
nativity's cathedral,

lie fighting men,
and praying men,
warmed by each others' blood
and the nighttime sweat
of tired vigilance.

They are surrounded by the keepers of Zion
those seen,
and those unseen.

And their harmony together
is found in rounds of fire
and occupation
seeing occupation
and resistance of each other.

Today, I saw a white clothed nun,
scurry like a frightened animal
past a green cloaked tank.

Her prayers, I'm sure,
are ones for safety for two troubled peoples,
for quiet ambles round Monday morning markets,
for stars of promise to
shine again in Bethlehem.

This strange country

Into this strange country
the godtree grew,
taking root in ground
we did not trust
finding nurture
in some other
earth
unrecognised by us.

And here,
among us
grew a life
that, by and by,
we recognised as living.

It discerned the
seasons in a
climate not our
own.

And, strangely,
it has shown us
shelter.

Its boughs
have made
our homes.

A reading from the book of exile chapter three

and he is inching towards glory
with only his own story on his back
he has patched up holes that opened
where his coverings have cracked
and some shoes were never meant for hiking so
he left them far behind
there are simple things he needs
on journeys such as these
food and love and drink and warmth and comfort
and a bag that's small enough
to carry all the failures and the idols
that he's picked up on the way

there are some days
he only moves
an inch or two

this is the pace of glory here in exile

L is for Lonely
(or, words to avoid when asked on a second date
'So . . . how've you been?')

L is for Lonely because that's what I've been.

O is for Ordinary because these days, it seems to me
loneliness is ordinary and ordinary's fine, and
ordinary is going to be here for a while.

N is for the Nothing, and the nothing's not lonely,
the lonely is just ordinary, but the nothing is void,
lonely, I can deal with, the ordinary's fine
but the nothing really scares me
with its deep vacant eyes.

E is for Everyone, because everyone's an 'I'
everyone's a little lonely, a little happy, a little shy,
everyone's an anyone
and anyone could be me
the poor and persecuted,
the pure and the meek.

L is for Licking the wound where I inscribed,
on my own skin, with my bloodink,
the yearning I can't hide.

Y is for Yonder, and yonder's not here
and right here is yonder to someone who's not here.
And yonder rhymes with wander

and wander rhymes with love
and all love's a little lonely
made with ordinary stuff.

The beginning of wisdom

was when I learnt the difference
between believing in the truth
and telling the truth
about
belief.

Flesh of my flesh

Flesh of my flesh
and bone of my bone
your skin is warm
and your hands are cold
warm them on me
warm them on me.
Let me look at you,
warm me on you.

My blood is red
it heats my skin
your skin is beautiful
it turns me into me.
Ah, have you burned
at the thought of me?
Like I have burned
when I am missing you.

I'd kiss your body
if you were close,
I'd kiss your lips
I'd cover most of your skin
with my love
with my breath.
with my yearning
for your flesh.

Northeast morning roads of home

On a cool November night,
we sat on broken chairs
on a winter's balcony
wrapped in old and holey blankets
and smelt the sulky storm, while
listening to the city's starlit skies,
speaking their own silence
to the sad and sinking storm inside your ribs.

Many moons have passed
and set on roofed horizons
since that quiet evening,
outside the empty flat,
with its unplugged fridge
and air of waiting for a springtime rustle.

At the sleepless dawning of
today, I passed that sultry
autumn balcony and saw
flickered lightning flashing
up the northeast morning roads of home.

'Tis the gift

'Tis the gift to be gentle
With your self at the end
of a day when you've given
of a day when you're spent.
To re-create, to breathe
and to rest
and to treat your own self
as your own
welcome guest

When hospitality's in place
you'll be kinder
to your self
and less inclined to haste.

You'll turn
and you'll fall
and you'll find
that you'll say

welcome to the night
and
welcome to the day.

Of skinny dipping, lonely nights, charcoal fires, absolution, loads of guilt, breakfast, bucketfuls of projection, and forgiveness (a longish reflection on the last chapter of the fourth gospel)

Dove, naked into cold water,
near the cove where the clothed man cooked fish.
The water was teeming with one hundred
and fifty-three screaming out
I do not know the man I do not know the man
I do not know the man whose shackled hands
I'd held the last time I'd seen the sea
walking towards me on Sophia's heels
stepping over chaos and creating madman's dreams.

One hundred and fifty three
and he a carpenter, telling me the fisher:
 'Cast your nets in the light of day'
So I explained that while I am a ragged man,
my sins are rich and meaty,
I would take a beating before I'd heard a carpenter
lay down the rules of eating from the sea.

One hundred and fifty three
and me, I followed,
because I knew no other way.
This was the way of glory,
the only way before me.
My wife she understood, or at least she kept her peace.
Seven score plus thirteen

leaping from the sea to nets so empty
they seemed dry.

Now I am leaping naked from the deck to sea
and me, I'm hoping for a bit of absolution
while I perform my oceanic ablutions.
I am naked ploughing depths of
wombing waters,
salty with my tears and years of
endless trying.

Three times of saying:
no, I do not know him, no, I do not know him, no, I do
not know him.
so can I show him anything that is different now?

He said 'hello'.
The carpenter, he said 'hello'
and I said 'Yeah, I know' pulling clothes around my body,
covering my hair and skin from showing.

Three times with bread and fish around a charcoal fire
and I was questioned of my love:
– do I love him more than fish?
more than all this? more than miracles? and me? and all
that's in me?

Jesus, you know everything I said,
and then I wept.
You know damnwell everything
I drank from miraculous new waters and then
I faltered while the devil sauntered downtown.
I am the pebble in your crown.
Jerusalem's new clown.

I've let you down,
I've let you down,
I've let you down,
I've left me damnwell down
Jesus, you know everything, I said,
and then I wept.

'Are we beyond all this?
can we move on?' he said.
'The miracles, big balled bravado
ah, your sad old ego vying for acceptance
are we beyond all this?
can we move on?' he said.

'Jesus you know everything
and the weight inside my head,'
I said.

And he said
'Come now, fisherman, come on
and maybe sing a different tune
and find a room where you can let me stay
and maybe take that oar out from your own eye
and paddle back to where I started with you.
Let's be beyond all this
and let's move on,' he said to me.

A reading from the book of exile chapter four

there are some things too meaningful for talking
and even feeling leaves us full of grief
at all we touch and need and
can never speak of

we are living lives that we can't state the name of
we are loving things that
we can never bear
we attempt belief in things that we can not explain
and we rest uneasy in this
sometimesseemingcruelgame

and we rest with tension so
beautiful
its heartaching

Creed

I once was blind but now I can see.
I once was him, but now I'm me.
I once was cold, but now I'm not.
I used to fear hell, where the fire is hot.
I wanted to be straight,
but the thing is I'm queer.
I thought I belonged there,
but I belong here.

I once was wrong,
because I thought I was right,
I thought that the darkness was the same as the night,
and thought that the light was consoling and beautiful
all it asked was:
 'be pure, and be right and be dutiful'.
But light can be insipid
and daytime can be vacuous,
and no cult is so crude as the cult of the miraculous.
I thought that walking on the water
would be the end of it all,
and addiction to articulation
was the start of my fall.

I fell into meaninglessness,
I fell into sin,
I fell into darkness, and I felt caged in,
and I fell into the arms of something that was lurking
in the corner,

in the shadows,
and it's been slowly converting
my methods and madness,
into myth and new meaning,
my sagas and sadness given girth
and given grieving.

And now I believe in the god of the human
the good and the glorious,
the generous and moving.

I once was blind,
now I'm blinder still
and inside my own nighttime,
I am silent and still.

The visit of the queen of the lesbians to the gay men's prayer group

When she came to visit
she said:
Don't ask me.
I'm just a driver.

When she came to visit
she said:
Questions reveal much
about the secrets of the questioner.

When she came to visit she said:
Ask a better question lads.

She said:
Misogyny is no
respector of your
homo-andro-centric
little worldwinds.

When she came to visit she said:
Just because you don't want to screw us
Doesn't mean you don't screw us.

So,
don't ask me to visit you.
Answer your own queries, queeries.

When she came to visit she said:
Cook for us instead.

That's what the queen of the lesbians said.

A song of ascent

This slope is not slippery
it is steep
and we
are at the feet
of a
great endeavour.

You need not fear
a dangerous descent.
because this ascent will
demand
enough
attention.

And if we slip
let us hope that
our grips
are
firm.

Our muscles will burn and ache.

In time,
perhaps we will find ourselves
upon a plateau
showing us
where we've come from
and

where we might be going
provided
we keep going.

Dominic and Jenny's sex life

I saw them dancing
and I ceased to wonder.
The thunder of his broadened shoulders
and her fine head held high, defiant
caring and care free.
She is his racing pegasus and he her
circling eagle.

If they were strangers
their pulse would draw them inward,
were they asunder
oh, I am sure that their
thunder and their lightning would
bring about a Holy Storm,
a Rain-Me-Down Storm,
a Flood-the-Earth-With-Water-and
Float-Upon-the-Ark-of-
Our-Own-Love Storm.

And they went in,
these two by two
and came out with these two more.

They have two beautiful small boys,
two joys of their existence,
each other of their own choosing,
but these boys of their
own Making.

Each owns the other and the other
knows his own
and they have recklessly demanded,
and received, the fruit
of all attention.

Oh, I watched them dancing
and I stopped to ponder
the fonder then I grew of this couple's
funky grooves.
With rhythm in his tender boots
and she exulting in the love that she is living
the life that she is loving.
Oh, I give you all my rage and my affection
my love and resurrection dreams.
I fling my hands up in the air
I have no cares upon me now
I dance around your body
and we are made here in this space,
born again to our own worlds,
hurled upon this
Dance Floor Centre Stage.

Because we are wounded and we are walking
and we are woken to the beat of our own force.

They own their Earth.
They Shape their Clay.
They Scale these Walls.
They make their Day.

I saw them dancing and I ceased to wonder.

Howth's soft heather

At my mother's prayer group on a Wednesday night,
some of the ladies fall asleep
from time to time
from bead to bead
from prayer to prayer.
They call it a holy sleep, thus sanctifying their little dozes.
Even the fire respects those sacred snoozes,
settling down comfortably to the business of glowing
gently, strongly, silently.

Twelve warm bodies in a cosy fire-lit den,
near the harbour and the old circus site.

'A Holy Sleep that brings supernatural rest and renewal'
A kind of coma into which you slip, mid prayer
and emerge, post trauma, spiritually nurtured,
to the gentle rhythm of clicking rosaries,
intoned voices,
century's prayers.

There are silent presences watching
those asleep and those awake,
hearing all those needs you daren't pray aloud
(for fear of clicking cups on saucers a coffee-morning
later).
They are watching those we love and those we hate to
leave
and hearing all those prayers voiced again,

just like last Wednesday,
for healing and a hope to find a kindly face.

And the sacred thing about this sleep
is that it is thus called,
thus loved,
thus recognised and welcomed,
like a snooze on Howth's soft heather
on a hot sunny September afternoon
by twelve lonely souls
who are looking towards the chat,
and the biscuits waiting on the pressed white cloth,
and hoping
that their fire will burn more bright.

Mo sheasamh ort, lá na choise tinne*

There are some things
that can't be stated quickly.
Only history
can meet us,
on the day when
our grief greets us.

It is only when I've
sailed across an ocean,
meeting you,
that I can meet you truly.
And I see
you in me
and the me in you
sees through me.

You are the place of standing
on days when feet are sore.
You are the harbour's landing
on days of the waves roar.
You are the arms enfolding
when I reject my flesh.
You are my gentle breathing
when I have lost my breath.

---

* An Irish phrase, used in parts of the Dingle Peninsula to indicate trust. It
translates as 'you are my standing on the day when my feet are sore'.

And sometimes,
though I have only met you
I know we've met before –
in a meeting of the eyes
there is the greeting
of a wise kind of knowing.

And it shows us that a family
is grown on samesuch moments:
the cleaving,
the leaving,
the making of some meaning in some exile,
the naming of that nameless thing,
the kind of sight that
brings believing.

And so,
though the frighttime hinders,
the nighttime lingers longingly
for us to grow inside her,
and we will find her handsome,
rewarding
rich and full and lovely.
Wonderful and far above the other
opportunities for being
human.

And we will find her tough,
and we will roughly jostle
with this mother,
desperately wishing for another
way for birthing out our living.

But she is giving us our own selves.
And we might live to tell the tale.

And we will find our family
on the day when the gale takes us

into harbour,
into shelter,
into holding,
into home.

A reading from the book of exile chapter five

he has grown older here.

the body speaks its own
language
and
he has started listening.

My love is a wide wide ocean

My love is a wide wide ocean
and I have wandered far from oceans.
I've forgotten how the waves are
made from skylight movements.
I am thirsting for the moment
when I'll find the other shore.
My love is a wide, wide ocean
and these inland, island roads I've taken
will not turn around.

I long for quiet minutes
by evening, or by morning
when sun, or moon, or stars,
or wind, or seagulls' heavy cries
will calm my mind to listen
will smooth this inside twisting
to feel the ocean's heartroll
in the dryland
of my breathing.

My love is a wide wide ocean,
and I am made for swimming.

I need to find some shores, some love,
by nighttime
or by day.

Ar eagla na heagla*

There is your fear
and your fear of your fear.

There is your beginning
and your fear of where you are.

There is your body
and your words about your body.

There is your possibility
and your hatred of all failure.

There is the gaze
and your fear of the gaze.

There is your destination
and your fear of where you're not.

---

* An Irish phrase, literally translated 'for fear of fear', but used in a similar
way to the English phrase 'just in case'.

Solitary flights

If I was a father, I would always carry sweets for flights
like this,
to ease the popping of my three children's ears.
It would be a memory in their minds when they, in turn
would buckle the belts of their own children,
check the exits,
and spread their fingers on their faces, touching cheek,
chin and lips
just like I do.

I sneeze just like my own father
and when I close my eyes,
and feel the sweet tickle of pain
through explosion of ears and nose,
I hear him,
in the sitting room, alone
like he is most nights,
watching telly,
or knelt at the chair with his book of evening prayer.

If I interrupted, the room would smell of him.
He'd ask if I wanted anything and I would say no,
I'd go to sleep,
and he'd go to a night of fitful dozing.
I'd hear his sleepless breathing
when I padded to the toilet in the dark,
locking the door behind me,
a habit of old I've not grown out of.

If I had children, I would number them three,
one, two, three.
A little trinity of souls,
with small shoes
and left-over crusts in their lunch-boxes,
long chins like mine,
maybe curly hair and green eyes.
And I would hold onto memories
of finger painting and action songs
long after they'd grown into jobs, lives, homes,
and solitary flights
to places I've never been.

Mourning prayer

I

On the early morning flight
she fingers prayerbeads
from her childhood.
Jesus Christ
Jesus Christ
child of the living God
have mercy
on me . . .
a woman.

Discreet phonecalls
looking up the clinic on the
streetfinder
she places hand on belly –
her own skin
on
her own skin,
and can't believe the place she's in.

II

Locating the church
two streets away
she lights candles
kisses icons
leaves her bag near the door
once more touching flesh
on flesh
and she faces walls of holy windows
feels the feelings
she cannot describe.

relief
exhaustion

alone.

III

Jesus Christ.
Sweet Jesus Christ,
dying son of the living God.
Have mercy on me
because
You need to.

Son of God,
who never had a womb;

here's my prayer,
offered with empty hands
and screaming;

here's my prayer
of opinions
and of meaning;

hear my prayer,
my reasons
my heartdreaming.

Binding the void with a name

You are finding, now,
belovéd,
the path to your own binding.

The footpath is paved
with the substitutes for
love and holding.

All those paperthin approvals
have been folding into themselves
for a long while now.

And it's not like it's dark.
it's just that there's no light.

Or, rather,
you cannot remember the light.

Or, even perhaps,
you cannot remember the feel of the light, belovéd.

Oh heavens above.
Oh chasm below.
Hither and thither.
Oh chaos composed.

So,
spill out the tumble
of your words.
They might be all you have left.

And,
Don't forget to
use them deftly.

In the absence of light
baptise the void
with a scalpelsharp insight,
and a name of
your choice.

An offering to God in exile

Based on the Hasidic tale from the Magid of Mezrich:

A king was overthrown and forced to travel as a wayfarer. He came to a house of poor people, who received him warmly, offered him shelter and shared their modest food. At the table, their hearts felt light and they all took delight in each other. Said the Magid – 'Now that God is in exile, so it is with God.'

Here is my open door.
Here is a warm welcome.

Here are my empty hands,
take delight in the touch of my skin.

There, your spoiled throne.
Here, a chair on which to rest.

Here, my blank books.
Enjoy the silence they create.

Here, dear one, some bread,
some cheese
and the last of last night's wine.
Let our hearts grow light
together at this table.

Here, our words.
Here, our listening.
Here, the gaze of our eyes, gazing.

Let us take pleasure
in each other.

A reading from the book of exile
the unwritable chapter

and the place of
pain
is the place of
survival
(and sometimes barely that)

Untitled # 1

Playing howling games
to see who hurts the most
– me, or my old heart.

Till death do us part

Neither of them died
but yet death
parted them.

No one should stand
at the grave
of their child.

Neither of them died
but yet
death
parted
them.

Intercession for lesbian and gay Ugandans

This is not a liberal agenda
Think about the people in the prisons in Uganda.

These are bodies like yours,
mine.
Close your eyes, please
close them.
Do not open them until you've breathed a little deeper.
Put the fingers of your one hand
to the wrist of the other
and keep your pulse a moment.

Are you calm?
Are you content in holding your own skin
with your own safe and holy skin?

Think about the people sleeping in the prison in Uganda.
This is not a liberal agenda.

These are people.
not quite corpses . . . yet

And it's not about forgetting
all your morals
with some rationalist adjustment
or some sad subjective judgment.

The Samaritan did not sin
yet still was hated,
berated,
judged and deemed a lesser kind of human.

Think about the people,
sleeping in the prison in Uganda.

This is not some liberal agenda.

Postcards to a dead friend

Since you died,
I've wondered where you are,
questioned hell and threatened heaven.
Is there a place for those who say they don't believe?
When you were sixteen,
you said that you'd believe when you were older,
maybe forty.
You barely got half way.

Since you died,
I think about my growing years differently.
How dare you
take my memories and paint them
with the bitter vinegar of your sad sorrows?
I had enough already.

Since you died,
I see your parents differently.
Solitary walks do not mean peaceful rambles,
and framed photographs are not artistic expression.
They looked like they'd been winded for months.

Since you died,
I've thought about you
more than I had in years.
Called you a dickhead most often,
and lurched at what caused
your final purging.

Since you died,
you will grow no older now –
the twenty-four year old Peter Pan
of your mother's mind.
Her lost boy,
caught in the never-never land
between the grave and the sky.

September the twelfth two thousand and one

In the wake of New York disaster
you slept,
curled up and hidden.

As ashes snowed down
On the streets of Manhattan,
you were covered by a white blanket.

You sleep like a child, my friend,
curled up and comforted by
soothing voices
and dreams of something else.

As adults weep,
and babies
wake and smile,
a long way down,
in the places of my breaking,

I pause a while,
and take some time to
think of cruelty,
and breathe.

Marbh is imithe ar mean lá an t-samhraidh*

Midsummers day.
'Good weather for a funeral'
– it was.

Twenty hours of grey,
the most grey that the season could offer,
and us standing soaked
in the wetness of it all,
damp and sodden, in the peaty graveyard,
winter boots on summer feet
on the longest bloody day,
more hours to hold more grey
than any other day.

And his fiancée was wailing in a most
god
awful
way.
Raw and unadulterated, unaccommodating the pain
that will stay and punctuate every single day,
and his mother, Jesus, his mother,
standing by a grave that Jesus didn't save her from.

Arms spread wide
this way
like some kind of crazy crucifixion.
– it was.

---

* Dead and gone on mid summers day

All is grey,
searching for meaning in this
meaningless day
praying for meaning
in the meaninglessness
of this meaningless mess.

He is gone,
Marbh 's imithe ar an lá seo, liath 's fluich
ó mo mhac, ochón, ochón, mo mhaicín brónach
uaigneach insan uaigh fhuar 's uaigneach.*

Today and every other day is now waked
by a grey absence,
bones frozen by clutch of dark earth.
No other way to stay in touch
besides reliving all that is now not living.

Count the calendar to anniversary days,
and count the unfair ways of living.

---

* dead and gone on this grey wet day oh my son, alas, alas my sad small
son, lonely in a cold and lonely grave

Untitled # 2

Christ of the rising tides
guide me in these seas
of risings and of fallings
and uncharted territories.

A reading from the book of exile chapter six

there is no ending.
everything is here.
> (so pitch a tent that you can live in
> and find a friend to whom you'll give
> in
> times of telling
> times of testing
> times of listening
> times of resting)

there is no ending.
everything is here.

A circle keeps beginning. A circle is unending.

A circle is spun,
a chord of sleep and breathing,
dreaming, unaware

[&]

if there is no end,
we need not fear hearts rending,
the circle is un . . .

Fashion the world
(for Wendy Musto)

Fashion the world in our image, we do,
us travellers two, with pains aplenty.
And pictures made, of the hearts in the shade
of the powerful, proud and the lonely.

Creating a world in our image we try,
I try, my arrogant past-time,
Moulding our friends to our heartbeats, we wished,
sometimes missed the last train homebound.

Beckoning God in our own ways, we flounder,
but now we've found a permanent Jesus.
He sees us, he leaves us to grow up believing
in this oxymoronic hope.

Fasten your seatbelt tightly, nightly,
this ride will leave you not breathing.
Caress all these talkings so lightly, this might be
our hearts speaking dreams we've not told.

Shhhhh

Quietly now,
for she is very near.

And though she doesn't frighten easily,
you must know
by now
that
you do.

What I needed to hear

This is my gift to you
this springtime blooming
this endless moving
from life to deeper life.

I will be your endlessness.
Your journey's start
and happy welcome home.
Your never ceasing,
always shining moment

Caught up in the wink of eternity,
you will be like you
have always been before,
never knowing.

A decade of sunset evenings
and the softest mornings dawnings
to bathe your tender brow
with healings of the deepest kind.

Narrative theology # 3

Open up this way of listening
to almighty echoes
in the caverns of my reading
in the hillsides of my ways.

A new way of listening
to the order and the chaos.
A mess can carry beauty
and a yearning bears its source.

May the rivers of our aching
know their force and mend their rending.

Oh the nighttime of our longing
waits for morning, waits for dawn.

The echo of a voice
finds room within my rooms
finds voice within my feeling
finds calm within my prayer.

Oh my lifetime, oh my waiting
oh my safe way through my caves.
Oh my Jesus in my nighttime
oh my walking on the waves.

Hold yourself together and pull yourself apart

*In a time of desolation do not make a life-changing decision
and do not go back on a decision made during a time of
consolation. Remember the times of consolation.
Ignatius of Loyola.*

Remember that this has passed before
and that there will be more days
of plenty . . . eventually.

Pay attention to your feelings
keep those feelings sharp.
Try to hold yourself together
and pull yourself apart.
Keep your eyes on the prize
that you might never gain.

Don't ignore whatever pain is blooming
like a flower that you never planted.
Occupy your hands with kindness.
Remember you can see, even though this blindness
is remarkable.

Mark the places that you're feeling
mark the spaces where you're needing held
mark the evenings that are dark
and mark the afternoon of coping.

Mark the morning that you waken
finding mourning has been taken
to a different part of heartland.

Remember what has passed before.
Pour your body like the sacramental wine
pour your blood with loving.

While he was in Malta

Ynohtna Luap is how you say
my Derry City lover's name
backwards.

It is with such thoughts as these
that I occupy my mind
when I'm
not with him.

And when I'm with him,
it is like the slipping in-between
the seconds
lighting little candles
on the glossy leaves of woodland.

Meanwhile,
I'm remembering with
memory of softhand touch.

His self holding
my
self
holding his own self.
saying very much and
very little
at the sametime.

Evol
is the way you say
the way I feel
towards him
backwards.

Who do you say that I am?

I

You say it's unnatural.
Yet when I speak of girlbirds loving girlbirds
or boybirds loving boybirds,
you say:
Why are you talking about animals?
Is that how you see yourself?

II

And as for Sodom,
you speak with no regard for Lot's daughters,
or all those lost voices in the unreported Abu Ghraibs
of our most recent century.

III

So,
how are we to talk
while we travel with each other?

IV

I, for one, will carve my own fury into a pencil
and scribble midrash on the map for our shared future
hoping you might learn the names
of places you've never seen.

V

So, listen.

Sex and the text
are strange things surely.

What we read and
the way we read
are two different things.

Let us hope that
lies be undone
and untruth be told out loud

so that a path may be revealed
before us.

Ar scáth a chéile a mhaireas na daoine*

I was sick for nine years.

And, during those nine years, I grew tired of offers of prayer for healing.

Eventually, far too late, I said: Please – I cannot handle your prayers. I am too tired to cope and too furious to hope for the things that you say so easily.

So, some friends prayed without me.

They sent me to a cabin near the sea,
they gave me wine, and timber for a fire.
they gave me silence, and space and grieving.

I took a walk every day and prayed the rosary and swore.
In the evening, I poured a glass of wine and cooked a
meal. I watched television and I watched the fire. I slept.

I believe that echoes
need a certain kind of emptiness
in order to be heard.

It is in the shelter of each other that the people live.

---

* An Irish saying meaning 'It is in the shelter of each other that the people live'.

The task is ended

The task is ended.
Go in pieces.

Our faith has been rear ended
certainty amended
and something might be mended
that we didn't know was torn.

And we are fire.
Bright, burning fire,
turning from the higher places
from which we fell,

emptying ourselves into the
hell
in which we'll find
our loving, and beloved
brother
mother
sister
father
friend

And so, friends, the task is ended.
Go in pieces
to see
and feel your world.

CPSIA information can be obtained
at www.ICGtesting.com
Printed in the USA
BVHW040519090419
544985BV00013B/213/P